INTRODUCTION

Peaky Blinders creator Steven Knight grew up in Birmingham in the 1960s and tells the story of how as a child he was sent to an address in a Small Heath street where men were sat round a table counting money. It's the starting point for the drama that has gripped a world audience – the illegal bookies run by the Shelby brothers in Watery Lane expands to become the Shelby Company and its boss, Thomas Shelby MP.

The series is set in the turbulent 1920s, with all the social and industrial upheaval following World War I. Knight has skilfully incorporated real-life figures into his drama, the Peaky Blinders were indeed a Birmingham gang, but from the late Victorian period, while Billy Kimber was a real-life gangster, but from nearby Aston and in charge of a violent gang known as 'the Birmingham Boys' who wanted to take control of racetrack betting.

Sadly, for a proud Brummie like Knight, many of the locations he needed to film a series around the city dubbed 'Britain's workshop' had disappeared in urban regeneration schemes. So the producers were forced to go further north and use the industrial heritage of Liverpool, Manchester and Bradford as backdrops – and the countryside of Yorkshire, Cheshire and Lancashire stood in for Birmingham's home county Warwickshire.

This location guide reveals some of the fabulous places used in *Peaky Blinders* from stately homes to old tobacco warehouses – from the banks of the River Wharfe in Yorkshire, to the side of the Shropshire Union Canal in Ellesmere Port. Almost all can be visited by fans who want to retrace the footsteps of Polly, Grace, Arthur, John, Ada and Michael, but sadly not the Digbeth Kid. Powis Street, which stood in for Watery Lane, has been returned to Liverpool Council and its terraced housing refurbished for urban rental. The site at the heart of it all, Uncle Charlie's scrapyard by the canal, is the Black Country Living Museum in Dudley and is open all year round, while Arley Hall in Cheshire, once famed for its beautiful borders and owned by Viscount Ashbrook, will forever belong to Tommy Shelby.

ABOVE
One of the original canal loading wharves.

RIGHT
A familiar meeting place for Ada and Freddie Thorne in Series 1.

FAR RIGHT
Tommy Shelby regularly uses Charlie Strong's yard to house anything from Scotch Whisky to horses. In Series 4, Aberama Gold tries to buy the yard, but backs down from a coin toss that could hand it to him.

BLACK COUNTRY LIVING MUSEUM
DUDLEY

One of the most recognisable locations in Peaky Blinders is Uncle Charlie's canalside yard, where Charlie and Curly hang out and offer wise counsel – advice that Tommy Shelby regularly ignores. It is a useful meeting place, storage facility and transit point for the slow journey down the Birmingham Canal Navigations to Camden Town in London. It is where Tommy dispenses summary justice to Danny 'Whizzbang' in the first series, where Arthur and John have a meeting with fatal consequences with the agitated Vincente Changretta, and where May Carleton arrives by canal barge in Series 4, half-suspecting that Tommy has arranged her transport for his own amusement.

The yard is part of the Black Country Living Museum in Dudley in the West Midlands, one of the very few locations close to where *Peaky Blinders* is actually set. With its canal bridges and historic industrial architecture, it provides other locations too. In series one, Ada and Freddie Thorne's snatched meetings occurred by the canal bridge, the same bridge that Finn trains his gun on while expecting an attack from the Changrettas. Down one of the

canal arms is a set of old lime kilns and in Series 4 Tommy takes Lizzie for a stroll there, thinking back to the time before France when this would be his romantic rendezvous spot.

The outstanding museum, which opened in 1978, was set up to showcase the industrial heritage of the West Midlands, in particular the Black Country which was at the heart of the industrial revolution of the 18th and 19th centuries. The boroughs of Dudley, Sandwell, Walsall and the city of Wolverhampton make up the Black Country to the west of Birmingham. Since its opening, the former railway goods yard and coal-mining site has collected over 50 buildings that have been dismantled and reconstructed on the 26-acre site. Charlie's yard is just a small part of what is an immersive museum with demonstrators

portraying the lives that would have been lived between 1850 and 1950.

Electric trams and trolleybuses transport visitors from the entrance to the recreated village, which includes: St. James' Infants School (1842 relocated from Dudley), Providence Chapel (1828 relocated from Netherton) Cradley Heath Workers' Institute (1912), Gregory's General Store (1883 relocated from Old Hill), Hobbs and Sons fish and chip shop, Brook Street back-to-back houses (1850s relocated from Woodsetton) and the Bottle and Glass Inn – don't expect the Garrison. There are many vintage metal-working businesses that have been lovingly taken apart and reinstalled on the site, plus you can take to the water. An electrically-powered narrowboat operated by Dudley Canal Trust makes trips on the Dudley Canal and into the

Dudley Tunnel, the second-longest canal tunnel in the UK, running through fossil-encrusted limestone.

With a short winter break in December and January, the Black Country Museum is open for the rest of the year, with special events dotted through the calendar – such as a 1940s weekend, and *Peaky Blinders* nights where fans of the show can don their flat caps (no razor blades please) and party on the actual set of the show. These have been so successful that four were planned for September 2022.

NATIONAL WATERWAYS MUSEUM
ELLESMERE PORT

Peaky Blinders is the most canal-centric drama on British television and the Shelbys use it to transport illicit goods between Birmingham and Camden Town in North London. It's also as an inconspicuous means of arriving in the capital city. To get there, the Blinders would have to use the Grand Union Canal and take a loop up the Regents Canal, but shooting in Camden or even Birmingham's famous Gas Street Basin would have been too problematic. Instead, the producers opted to use the canalside buildings

at the National Waterways Museum in Ellesmere Port coupled with a heavy dose of CGI. If you are revisiting the episodes which show Black Country men unloading at Camden and making their way to Alfie Solomon's warehouse, look out for the metal bridge which some of them cross.

Designed by the great civil engineer Thomas Telford, Ellesmere Port was once the largest Inland Waterway dock complex in the UK. It stands on a junction of the Shropshire Union Canal

ABOVE
The metal steps and bridge at the Waterways Museum mark the point where the Birmingham men disembark in Camden Town.

TOP RIGHT
All aspects of Britain's canal heritage are gathered here, including beautifully restored commercial boats.

ABOVE RIGHT
Ellesmere basin lies at the end of the Shropshire Union Canal where it meets the Manchester Ship Canal. It was a place for transshipping cargoes.

with the Manchester Ship Canal close to the River Mersey. In the past it was a vital transshipment hub where goods from Birmingham and Staffordshire could be transported to larger vessels and on to the rest of the world.

Today, the National Waterways Museum hosts many different exhibitions in its 19 Grade II-listed buildings but there are absolutely no large quantities of spirits in the Island Warehouse. Almost 90% of the UK's inland waterways collections are gathered here, and that includes 50 boats. Not all would have fitted on the Grand Union or the Shropshire Union. *Basuto*, one of the few remaining Clyde Puffers (of *Para Handy* fame) built in

1902, would be more at home on the Crinan Canal in Scotland. There are smaller boats, such as the *Starvationer*, a wooden-built narrow craft (with exposed ribs on the outside) used in the 1800s by the Worsley coal mines near Manchester. There are many boats which contributed to the nation's industrial heritage – dredgers, tugs and ice-breakers along with classic leisure craft and a range of narrow boats. The museum is open for a large part of the year – and if you really want to see a collection of the best-preserved and turned out boats, the annual Easter Gathering (which sounds like the Lee family afloat) is the time to visit.

ARLEY HALL
NORTHWICH, CHESHIRE

Up until the release of season three of *Peaky Blinders*, Arley Hall, near Northwich in Cheshire, was famous for its magnificent garden and Grade I- and II-listed buildings. That all changed when Tommy Shelby moved in. Though the celebrated herbaceous borders and 1845 mansion built with Hollington stone were famous on a national scale, *Peaky Blinders* has made Arley Hall internationally famous.

For plot purposes, it is Arrow House, not far from Stratford upon Avon in Warwickshire, thus within motoring distance of the Shelbys' territory in Small Heath. The rumbustious wedding party sets the tone of what the household staff can expect from the new owner – there is no similarity between the parties thrown by Thomas Shelby and, say, *Downton Abbey*'s Earl of Grantham.

The house is witness to the traumatic events of Series 3, and its abandonment for a return to Watery Lane in Series 4 when Luca Changretta – who is staying at the Inkberrow Hotel in Stratford upon Avon – gets too close for comfort. Indeed, the Arley Estate was used for the scene in Episode 4 when Luca's Rolls-Royce is delayed by a road block and Aberama Gold misses out on the opportunity to neutralise the threat from the mob.

Script Executive Bryony Arnold told the *Warrington Guardian* why the production crew enjoyed coming back to the Hall: "What we love about somewhere like Arley is its authenticity. That's stuff you can't recreate necessarily in a studio. It's having that sense of freedom of movement. So for example, for Tommy and Grace's wedding we had lots of long moving shots between rooms and we were following characters as they moved through. That's really difficult to achieve when you're in a studio."

ABOVE LEFT
A view along the Furlong Walk at Arley Hall.

ABOVE
The wedding night boxing match between the Blinders and the Military was set against Arley's magnificent topiary.

However the producers didn't want too grand a house for Tommy. "This is a man who has now accumulated a lot of wealth but he's not very grandiose so we had to find this middle balance of feeling like he's gone up in the echelons of society but also for it not to feel like a Buckingham Palace-equivalent for example."

Arley Hall may not be fit for a king but it was fit for an emperor. The Emperor's Room is where Napoleon III (nephew of Napoleon Bonaparte) stayed in the winter of 1847-48 during a period of exile in England before returning to France and political power. It has been preserved in its original form and is just one of the many attractions visitors can see at Arley. These include the Furlong Walk in the 12 acres of garden and in which a marquee was erected in Series 5 to host the ballet attended by Oswald Mosley.

CHATSWORTH HOUSE
DERBYSHIRE

When aristocratic horse trainer May Carleton takes a shine to Tommy Shelby at a horse auction it's the start of something big. For Tommy it's part of an ambitious plan to take control of betting on racecourses in the south of England; for May – widowed by the Great War – it's a flirtation with a bad boy gangster to bring excitement into her life. With a bit of horse training thrown in as well.

The grand stately home used to portray Mrs. Carleton's estate is Chatsworth House in Derbyshire, home to the Duke and Duchess of Devonshire. Apart from Tommy Shelby – Mary Queen of Scots, Queen Victoria, Prince Albert and Charles Dickens have enjoyed overnight stays on the estate that has been in the Cavendish family since 1549.

It was also home to the notorious and celebrated Georgiana Spencer, a distant relation to Lady Diana Spencer, who married the 5th Duke of Devonshire in 1774 and was the subject of the film *The Duchess* starring Keira Knightley. Naturally the film was shot at Chatsworth, as was Keira Knightley's version of the Jane Austen classic *Pride and Prejudice,* where the house doubled for Mr. Darcy's magnificent Pemberley.

ABOVE
Filming for Series 2 of *Peaky Blinders* took place in the summer of 2014 with scenes in the grounds, the stables, the Painted Hall, Library, Guest Bedrooms and the Great Dining Room..

LEFT
The Library at Chatsworth House.

THE PLAZA CINEMA
STOCKPORT

There is a tenuous link between these two *Peaky Blinders* locations as the Plaza in Stockport was used to portray an assassination attempt on Oswald Mosley in Series 5. Mosley was married to Diana Mitford. Deborah Mitford, the youngest of the six famous Mitford sisters (Diana, Nancy, Unity, Jessica and Pamela), was married to the 11th Duke of Devonshire, whose home was Chatsworth.

The Plaza Cinema in Stockport was opened in 1932. It's a Grade II-listed building and a favourite of cinema buffs, particularly cinema organ buffs because it has an original Compton cinema organ. Enthusiasts get all steamed up about the unique 150-stop tab layout, the 42 toe and thumb pistons, and the 11 ranks of pipes situated in 2 chambers to the right of the stage. It was used as a Mecca bingo hall until 1999. A National Lottery grant helped fund a £1.9m restoration in 2009 to restore many of its 1932 features and today is known as The Plaza Super Cinema and Variety Theatre.

ABOVE
An Art Deco jewel that has been lovingly restored.

LEFT
The Plaza was used as Bingley Hall in Birmingham, Britain's first purpose-built exhibition hall (1850). Although it was used for a variety of annual shows, boxing matches and industrial exhibitions, the cavernous interior was also used for political rallies. It was burned down during the 1984 Midland Caravan and Camping Show and replaced by the International Convention Centre (ICC).

PORT SUNLIGHT

THE WIRRAL

Although at one point in *Peaky Blinders* Tommy Shelby reflects, "What Polly wants will always be a mystery to me," he does get one decision right. In Episode 2 of Series 2 he takes Polly to a house in Sutton Coldfield and reveals that he's bought it for her.

Fully furnished, her new residence is in the mock Tudor style that came into fashion in the late 19th century, and Polly's house is part of a genteel neighbourhood far away from the grime of Watery Lane and Small Heath.

The house can be found in Park Road, Port Sunlight, and is one of 900 Grade II-listed buildings that make up the model industrial village set up by the Lever Brothers. Work on the village, which is in the Metropolitan Borough of Wirral, Merseyside, started in 1888, and continued all the way through to World War I. It was named Port Sunlight after the Sunlight soap brand which was one of the company's leading products, and ironically the location is almost directly opposite Powis Street, the Liverpool street used to portray Watery Lane, on the other side of the Mersey.

RIGHT
The house on Park Road originally occupied by Lord Leverhulme is now a community hub.

BELOW
Polly's new house is a step up from the back-to-backs of Small Heath.

RIGHT
The bridge over The Dell with the Lyceum spire beyond.

Because of rigorous planning restrictions, the facades of the houses and community buildings in Port Sunlight have remained very much as intended by their benefactor, and so other *Peaky Blinders* scenes have been filmed nearby. In fact just across the road from Polly is The Dell, a parkland walk that was the scene of a potential assassination in Series 3, when Tommy has his sights set on Father Hughes. The bridge that crosses The Dell is a favourite spot for wedding photos. With the spire of the Lyceum Club visible beyond, Tommy sets off after his target in determined mood unaware that things are about to go horribly wrong.

Polly's house is also just a few yards up the road from Bridge Cottage, the original home of Lord Leverhulme (as he became) on the estate, and today the house is used as a community hub.

POWIS STREET
LIVERPOOL

The terraced streets of Small Heath in south-east Birmingham, are the setting for Peaky Blinders, with the Shelbys running their bookmakers out of knocked-through, two-up-two-down terraced houses in Watery Lane. Small Heath was the home of the BSA (British Small Arms) factory, and there was indeed a Watery Lane, which in past times was the site of a tollgate on the Birmingham to Coventry Turnpike. Watery Lane is no more, it was redeveloped as part of a ring road scheme, but so much of pre-war Birmingham has been redeveloped that the show's producers had to turn to the derelict streets of Liverpool to recreate Small Heath.

Powis Street in Liverpool's Toxteth district was the perfect fit for the Shelbys' centre of operations. It is part of a series of streets known as The Welsh Streets. They are a group of late-19th-century terraced streets built to house Welsh workers moving to Liverpool for employment and named after Welsh villages and valleys. Powis Street sits between Rhwilas Street and Madryn Street, where the Beatles Ringo

Starr was born and lived until the age of four.

The enclave, which also includes, Voelas, Kinmel, Gwydir, Pengwern and Treborth Streets was designed with wide roads and tree-lined pavements. Indeed, a historic image of Voelas Street shows a tree-lined terrace with young trees planted on both sides of the street. The whole area had declined with unemployment hitting Liverpool hard in the late 1970s and early 1980s, as portrayed by landmark TV series *Boys from the Black Stuff*. At the turn of the century the council decided they had enough historic terraced housing stock and that Ringo Starr's birthplace was not worthy of saving. Millions were spent rehousing the remaining residents and the Welsh Streets prepared for demolition, but the government funding was withdrawn in 2011 and so their fate was put on hold.

Enter Caryn Mandebach Productions who took over the now-resident-free Powis Street and painted the houses

black to represent soot-covered Small Heath. The terrace was used a lot in Series 1 and 2, less in 3 and 4. With Aunt Polly moving out to Sutton Coldfield and Tommy and Arthur moving up in the world, the Blinders left Watery Lane behind them as a place of residence, only returning in Series 4 under threat from the Changrettas. Now it will be impossible for them to return. Placefirst, a social housing company, has started renovating the streets, and though you can still walk down the road where Major Campbell galloped, the Lees lay in wait and where Tommy offered Lizzie an irresistible amount of money, it's now been transformed into some very attractive residences.

ST. GEORGE'S HALL
LIVERPOOL

When Grace meets Inspector Campbell in a Birmingham museum (Interiors from Newby Hall in Yorkshire) she walks in through an impressive colonnade. In the first series those Greek columns were rumoured to be Leeds Town Hall – but for Series 2 they were part of a building described by architectural critic Nikolaus Pevsner as, 'one of the finest neo-Grecian buildings in the world'.

St George's Hall opened in 1854 and has held rallies, concerts, exhibitions and became an enlistment station in the Great War. Prior to Charles Dickens sailing to America, on his second and final speaking tour, a banquet was hosted in the Great Hall for him. It is in that same hall that Grace Shelby received the bullet intended for Tommy Shelby and sent his world spinning into despair in one of the most heartbreaking scenes in *Peaky Blinders*. It is also used in Series 6 as the venue for an Oswald Mosley rally that Tommy and Lizzie attend.

BELOW
The neoclassical colonnades, typical of many US buildings of state, make St. George's a filming favourite. It can also be seen in The Batman (2022).

BOTTOM
The Great Hall, scene of a fateful charity gala.

SEACOMBE FERRY TERMINAL
WALLASEY, THE WIRRAL

Peaky Blinders fans travelling to Liverpool have a variety of different locations they can check out, but the Seacombe Ferry Terminal has been a tourist attraction long before the television series came on to our screens. Gerry Marsden's anthemic hit 'Ferry Cross the Mersey' from 1965 cemented Liverpool's place in pop culture of the 1960s, celebrating a ride on the ferry that started out from the Seacombe Ferry Terminal. Marsden, who was great friends with the Beatles and managed by Brian Epstein, was born in Menzies Street, Toxteth, not far from Powis Street where the series was filmed.

In Series 3, the Ferry Terminal doubled for Liverpool's Cunard Line transatlantic departure hall, where the Shelbys seek out Vincente Changretta before he can get on a liner to the United States. The consequences of the Blinders' actions that day will have far-reaching consequences in Series 4. The production crew had to repaint the Victorian linkspan bridge, which has been in use for over 130 years, in more muted colours and hang up some flags to emphasise the point that his was now a transatlantic terminal.

BELOW
Two views of the linkspan building leading to the Mersey ferry. The top image, as commuters and tourists view it; and below, decked out for a much longer crossing.

STANLEY DOCK

LIVERPOOL

The gritty industrial setting of the Garrison Tavern at the end of a broad alley of factories belching fire and smoke is well known to *Peaky Blinders* viewers. Set in the heart of manufacturing Birmingham (the workshop of Britain) the series makes much of this roadway set between factories – it's a great location for epic slow-motion walking shots. But the truth is, it's nowhere near Small Heath.

The lane in question is behind the Tobacco Warehouse at Stanley Dock in Liverpool. This 14-story Grade II-listed building dates to 1901 and is thought to be one of the biggest brick buildings in the world. Across the other side of Stanley Dock is the North Warehouse which opened in 1854. This is the setting for a confrontation between Freddie Thorne and Tommy Shelby as they discus Freddie's future, staring out across the expanse of Stanley Dock – a meeting that ends up with them pointing revolvers at each other a-la-*Reservoir Dogs*.

Today that site has been converted into the Titanic Hotel, part of the long-term redevelopment of the Liverpool docklands. This includes

ABOVE
With their backs to the Garrison, the Blinders face up to the better dressed Kimber gang.

RIGHT
The warehouse on the left is now the Titanic Hotel. Tommy and Freddie faced off by the first archway.

FAR RIGHT
An image looking the other way down 'Garrison Lane' taken in 2012 before the Blinders arrived. This view is from where the Garrison tavern would be. If you look at the windows and doorways above Arthur's head on the top image, they match up to windows and doorways to the left of this photo.

THE GARRISON

The real Peaky Blinders gang existed in Birmingham in the late Victorian era, an earlier time period than the television series. They were rumoured to meet in The Garrison pub which can still be found across from Garrison Park on Garrison Lane in Small Heath. Sadly it closed in 2014, just as the fictionalised Blinders started to gain worldwide notoriety. It was sold at auction for £183,000 to a developer who wanted to turn the Victorian building into flats. Planning permission was re-fused and there might be future plans to re-open it as a Blinders-themed pub, and by order of Arthur, the only Blinders pub with a genuine claim to the name.

the Tobacco Warehouse which is due to be converted into 538 apartments with 100,000 square feet of commercial space on the ground floor. You will soon be able to stroll down the street

where the Blinders faced off with Billy Kimber's gang, and where two perambulators were pushed with their explosive contents.

RODNEY STREET
FALKNER SQUARE
GLADSTONE PAVILION

LIVERPOOL

The area of Liverpool under the postcode Liverpool 8 (Ringo Starr released an album of the same name) is also known as Toxteth – and while there are the working-class houses in the Welsh Streets, there are also some upmarket residences too.

Falkner Square

When Tommy is tasked with killing Henry Russell, a particularly brutal British Field Marshal, the plan is to make his London home uninhabitable. John Shelby duly delivers an explosive package through the front door while Johnny Dogs keeps the policeman stationed outside talking.

The Blinders didn't have to go far to find a suitable residence. The house exterior used was in Falkner Square, Toxteth, part of Liverpool's Georgian Quarter and a short walk from Rodney Street.

Rodney Street

Tommy buys his sister Ada a London townhouse, with the vague idea that he might be able to station some of his men there in his push into London. Ada's having none of it, though she does take in a student lodger who proves very useful to Thomas in the final episode of Series 2, when he takes him along to Alfie Solomons' warehouse.

In real-life Ada's house belongs to Peter Wood, who welcomes film crews into his house in Rodney Street, Liverpool. The location has been used before as Harley Street consulting rooms in *The Forsyte Saga*, and as a 1940s home in *Close to the Enemy*. When film crews move in they transform the house, not only filling the house with period-appropriate furniture, but redecorating and recarpeting. Once filming is over

ABOVE
Ada's London gaff in Liverpool's Rodney Street.

ABOVE RIGHT
The Isla Gladstone Pavilion in Stanley Park. Today it is used for a variety of purposes, wedding hire and to provide hospitality packages for Liverpool Football Club, which is the closer of the two Premiership sides.

the production crew return the house to its original condition. Neighbours will be paid too for the inconvenience of having a load of filming gazebos outside on the pavement.

Isla Gladstone Pavilion

In the frantic final episode of Series 2 Tommy's horse is running in The Derby at Epsom, in south-west London. But with the production shooting in the north-west, coupled with the fact that Epsom has lost its Victorian buildings, an alternative needed to be found. The producers settled on a location midway between two of Britain's greatest sporting venues, Anfield and Goodison Park. Stanley Park, the location of the pavilion, was opened in 1870 when it was on the northerly edge of the city. The intention by designer Edward Kemp was to recreate a park for exercise and fresh air, with the pavilion a conservatory housing tropical plants grown in nearby greenhouses.

The Isla Gladstone Pavilion was gifted to the park by Alderman Henry Yates Thompson in 1900. Thompson had

built an even grander glasshouse, the Palm House, in Sefton Park in the south of the city, so this was very much evening out his citywide largesse. The Palm House was restored in 2000 and provided a model for the restoration of the Gladstone Conservatory, which had long fallen into disrepair and been boarded up.

BOLTON

LE MANS CRESCENT AND ST. PETER'S CHURCH

When the Peaky Blinders decide to expand their operations south in Series 2, that means taking on the Sabini gang in London. Tommy, Arthur and John make a big show of turning up to Sabini's jazz club, located on an elegant Georgian-style crescent. It's also the place where Tommy approaches Ada, who's now living in a London townhouse with an upper class student lodger (actor Josh O'Connor who would go on to play Prince Charles in *The Crown*) to persuade her to come home. In reality, the upmarket crescent location is far from Sabini's territory in the capital city – it's in Bolton, Lancashire, behind the town hall.

Le Mans Crescent was designed by Bolton architects Bradshaw, Gass and Hope after the council decided to build a new civic centre in 1923. Once the area of Howell Croft and Spring Gardens was cleared, work began on the neoclassical crescent, which would hold a central library, art gallery,

museum, magistrates court and police station, in 1932. Thus the building is actually slightly younger than the time period in which it is portrayed.

The Magistrates Court closed in 2017 when cases moved to Bolton Crown Court, however the rest of the council facilities, such as the museum, art gallery and library continue. There are plans to turn the old court building into an 87-room hotel, though not before further filming had wrapped for Series 6. The production crew returned at the end of March 2021 when the building was used as the Grace Shelby Sanatorium for Sick Children where daughter Ruby is being treated.

Across town in Bolton-le-Moors, St. Peter's Church, otherwise known as Bolton Parish Church, is the setting for a meeting between Tommy and Arthur's wife, the God-fearing Linda Shelby, in the penultimate episode of Series 6. With Arthur going rapidly

downhill Tommy wants to know if there is forgiveness for Arthur. Linda can't find it in her heart to forgive him, but the good news is that God should be willing to give it a go.

The name parish church belies St. Peter's impressive size. It has the highest parish church tower in Lancashire 55m (180 feet) and is believed to be the fourth church on the spot. When its 15th-century predecessor was demolished, and foundations dug for the new church, remains of an Anglo-Saxon church and a Norman Church were found.

LONDON ROAD FIRE STATION
MANCHESTER

Tommy Shelby's days look numbered when he is followed by a truckload of Luca Changretta's men who tail his grey Bentley after a visit to see Michael Gray in hospital. It looks like Polly has betrayed Tommy... except it's all a plan to draw the Italian mobster out. Episode 5 of Series 4 contains an epic gun battle as Tommy leads his pursuers into the courtyard of the London Road Fire Station in Manchester and proceeds to uncover a series of weapons that he has carefully concealed in advance.

At the time of filming, the abandoned fire station was awaiting approval of a development plan. Situated opposite Piccadilly Station in the centre of Manchester and opened in 1906, the triangular building was a showpiece for civic architecture, rich with glazed tiles, heroic sculptures and stained glass throughout – every bit the match for the Victoria Baths.

There were 38 flats for firemen and their families, a large Engine House for seven horse-drawn appliances, workshops, a social club, a gym/dance hall, a police station with seven cells, an ambulance station, and a small coroner's court. The *Manchester Guardian* said at the time of the £142,000 building: 'The great pile of buildings at London Road is an example of pride, beauty and practicality being utilised in the governance of a city. There is nothing

ABOVE LEFT
Tommy opens fire in the central courtyard.

ABOVE
The exterior of the building, soon to become a hotel.

RIGHT
How it looked in the 1950s with a large audience to watch the firemen practice their drills,

quite like it anywhere in the country and maybe beyond.' It served the city of Manchester for 80 years but was closed in 1986, while the Coroner's Court continued until 1998.

Since the visit of *Peaky Blinders*, development of the historic building has been approved and the space is being turned into a boutique hotel, an events space, with a variety of restaurants on the ground floor. No weapon caches.

VICTORIA BATHS
MANCHESTER

Manchester's classic Victoria Baths have provided the backdrop for more than one important scene in *Peaky Blinders*. It made its debut in Episode 3 of Series 1, when the sports hall was used as the auction ring for the thoroughbred sale. Tommy buys the grey that he will name Grace's Secret but has to pay over the odds after competition from May Carleton who later hands him her card and offers to train his new acquisition. It can also be seen in the early part of the final episode of season four, when Tommy and Alfie Solomons sit downstairs and talk during the Bonnie Gold versus Goliath boxing match, and when Arthur goes looking for an assassin.

There are many different aspects to the Baths including an Edwardian version of a hammam or Turkish Bath comprising three hot rooms with levels of rising heat – plus a wet steam room known as a Russian Bath. There is also a cooling room used to acclimatise customers after their 'treatment' and it is in these rooms that one of the most dramatic scenes in *Peaky Blinders* is played out.

The baths were opened in 1906 and the Lord Mayor of Manchester declared the buildings 'a water palace of which every citizen of Manchester is proud'. There were three swimming pools of varying size for use by 1st Class Males, 2nd Class Males, with the smallest being Females Only. The 1st Class

ABOVE
Tommy Shelby reacts to an ambush by the Sabini gang in the auction ring – the former 2nd Class Males swimming pool.

TOP RIGHT
The hammam room where Tommy and Alfie discuss the big fight.

ABOVE RIGHT
There's a bit of cheeky banter on the stairs from the Blinders after Tommy wins his horse at auction.

RIGHT
The main pool. Mixed bathing was only allowed after 1914, and then only for families.

Males, or Gala pool is the largest, and that, along with the Females pool, has retained its poolside cubicles.

Victoria Baths closed in 1993 and the building was left with minimal maintenance by the city council until the Friends of Victoria Baths stepped in to stop the rot. Most important of all the preservation initiatives, was the 2003 BBC series *Restoration*, which it won, attracting further grants from English Heritage and the Heritage Lottery Fund.

The 2nd Class Males pool has become the Sports Hall with its cubicles stripped out and a sprung dance floor installed across the pool area. Apart from hiring out the space to film production companies the venue is available for events between April and November, or for group tours of the buildings.

JOHN RYLANDS LIBRARY
MANCHESTER

It's rare to see Tommy Shelby in a library, unless it's the one at home at Arrow House/Arley Hall. However in Episode 2 of Series 3 he needed to find out some information about the Russians staying at the Wilderness House near Hampton Court. He goes to see his sister, Ada Thorne, who's spending her days working at an impressive academic library. Ada is curious about the Russian man who was at Tommy's wedding, but still hands over a book about the Revolution, adding sarcastically that it's about "the bastards that ran away". The library featured on screen was the John Rylands Research Library, an important Grade I-listed late-Victorian neo-Gothic building on Deansgate in Manchester. Opened to the public in 1900, it had been commissioned in 1890 by Enriqueta Augustina Rylands in memory of her husband, John Rylands and became part of the University of Manchester in 1972. That book on the Russian Revolution is probably still out and racking up fines.

LEE QUARRY
BACUP, LANCASHIRE

ABOVE
An aerial view shows the
variety of old workings
at Lee Quarry.

Throughout *Peaky Blinders* the Lee Family move around – as gypsies do – and in episode three of the final series, Tommy finds their encampment in a bleak part of the country. Sick with worry about his daughter Ruby he is looking for Esme, the widow of his brother John, keen to find information about the sapphire and the curse.

Ironically, the camp site the producers chose for the Lees was… Lee Quarry Country Park, close to Bacup in the Rossendale Valley. Stone was quarried at Lee Farm from around 1820 and throughout the 19th century right up until the 1990s when it was owned by Bardon Roadstone. Coupled with nearby Cragg Quarry it is now an active Mountain Bike Trail site, and

also a great place for dog walkers and historians searching out the relics of Rossendale's industrial heritage. Lancashire County Council bought the quarry and turned it into a country park, and so access is free.

BELOW
If you're a *Peaky Blinders* fan who likes mountain biking, you can take on the Red Route, which is around four miles long, or the trickier Black Route, which is just over half a mile long.

NORTHERN TOWN HALLS

Much is made of the 'Northern Powerhouse' today, but the locations used by *Peaky Blinders* across six series reveal what a powerhouse it was in the past, with both Manchester and Leeds Town Halls appearing in Series 1. The wealth generated by northern industrialists helped create impressive civic buildings across Lancashire and Yorkshire that have been employed in various guises. St. George's Hall in Liverpool played host to Grace's charity gala and the buildings in Le Mans Crescent (near the Sabini gang's Eden Club) are part of Bolton Town Hall. But there are more besides...

Stockport Town Hall
The panelled rooms of Stockport Town Hall were used as the Shelby Company boardroom for the tense meeting at the start of Series 5. Following the Wall Street crash and Michael Gray's failure to dispose of the company's stockholding, an emergency meeting needs to be held. Polly bowls in followed by Lizzie, and as the camera tracks back it reveals portraits of John, Tommy and Arthur at the far end of the room. Such was the allure of the Blinders by Series 5 that even a passing David Beckham couldn't resist nipping into Stockport Town Hall to get a selfie

with Tommy Shelby's painting on the wall behind him.

Rochdale Town Hall

The interior corridors of this Gothic Revival building are a perfect substitute for the most famous Gothic Revival structure of them all, the Houses of Parliament. And so when civil servants have to scurry down corridors in the direction of Winston Churchill – Rochdale Town Hall is used. The building was completed in 1871 just a year after the Palace of Westminster.

One of its key appearances was as the hall hosting the election count for the Birmingham South constituency, in the final episode of Series 4. An elated Shelby family entourage emerges after the 'aforesaid Thomas Shelby' emerges as the new Labour MP for the area.

Bradford City Hall

At the beginning of Series 4, after the majority of the Shelby family avoid the noose, an isolated Tommy Shelby prepares for a solitary Christmas. The camera follows him as he walks past a brass band playing outside the Midland Hotel, with a gaggle of small children singing carols on the steps. He walks into the grand lobby, upstairs to a table in the central atrium, lights a cigarette and waits for Lizzie to arrive. A more significant moment happens at the end of Episode 3 in Series 4 when Polly puts on a red evening dress and sits at the bar of the Midland Hotel with champagne. She is joined by Luca Changretta to whom she proposes an arrangement that will spare Arthur and Finn, but deliver Tommy to the Italian mobster. Both these scene were filmed in the 1873 Venetian Gothic building that regularly hosts film and television crews facilitated by Screen Yorkshire.

OPPOSITE
An exterior view of Bradford City Hall.

BELOW LEFT
Shades of Westminster in Rochdale Town Hall.

BELOW
The impressive atrium of Bradford City Hall doubling as the Midland Hotel.

BOTTOM
A tense Shelby Co. meeting in Stockport.

UNDERCLIFFE CEMETERY

Living such a violent life it is no surprise that the Peaky Blinders end up visiting a cemetery on a regular basis. Tommy Shelby is never one to waste an opportunity and, after he dispatches his former comrade in the Warwickshire Yeomanry, Danny Wizzbang; the grave is used to hide guns (or as Major/Inspector Campbell likes to call them "gons") stolen from BSA. It's also the scene of a fraught meeting between Polly and Freddie Thorne, and a similarly angry meeting where Mrs Ross, mother of the teenage victim of Arthur's boxing rage, rails at Tommy who is there to hand over money.

With a lot of Series 1 filmed in Yorkshire, one of the obvious choices for a graveyard location was the Undercliffe Cemetery in Bradford. Thanks to the income generated by Yorkshire mills in the 19th century, Bradford had been a wealthy city. Cotton cash generated the wealth to create 'Little Germany' a district of impressive Victorian buildings, one of which was used as Tommy's factory when he meets with Union Convener Jessie Eden in Series 4.

With all that 'brass' at their disposal, the families of local industrialists built some epic monuments and mausoleums for their earthly remains. And the place to do it was at Undercliffe which was run by the Bradford Cemetery Company of 1849. Two chapels were built on the hillside site in 1854, later enlarged in 1878 and one of the notable directors of the company was Titus Salt, responsible for a model industrial village at Saltaire, now a UNESCO World Heritage site.

In the 20th century, burials dwindled and with mounting costs for maintenance of the site, Bradford Council sold it to a property developer in 1980. Luckily the Land Registry refused to allow any building on consecrated ground and so the council took it back in 1984.

Today, the cemetery is run by a charitable organisation, the Undercliffe Cemetery Charity which arranges maintenance and also organises monthly tours throughout the year, highlighting different aspects of its history and its residents' lives. Access is free but a donation to the site maintenance is always welcome. You can be your own Tommy Shelby.

LEFT AND BELOW LEFT
Established on a hillside location, the atmospheric Victorian cemetery allows film crews to avoid 20th and 21st century buildings on the horizon.

BELOW
Aunt Polly, the incomparable Helen McCrory, has a feisty encounter in the cemetery with Freddie Thorne (Iddo Goldberg).

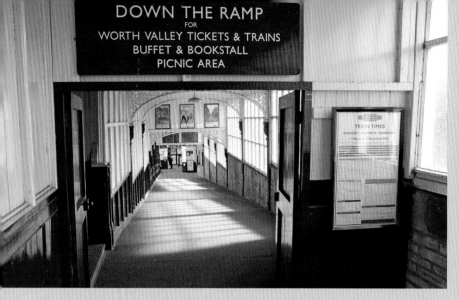

KEIGHLEY STATION
WEST YORKSHIRE

With the first series of *Peaky Blinders* backed by Screen Yorkshire, when it came to choosing a railway line for some pivotal scenes, the Keighley and Worth Valley Railway was the obvious choice. Keighley Station is unusual in that it has both a vintage side – with lines running up a five-mile stretch of the Worth Valley – and a Network Rail side, connecting to Leeds and Bradford in one direction, or Skipton in the other.

It featured prominently in the first series when Arthur Shelby confronted dad Arthur Senior after handing over a considerable sum of money to the bare knuckle fighter, expecting to sail to New York with him. Confrontation seems to be a regular theme at Keighley. Ada arrived there to tell Freddie Thorne (who is leaving the city under fear of being arrested) that she is pregnant with his child, and then there is the memorable cliffhanger at the end of Series 1 when Inspector Campbell threatens the departing Grace, and a shot rings out...

The branch line from Keighley was first proposed in 1861, when John McLandsborough, a civil engineer and fan of Charlotte Brontë's novels, visited Haworth, the home of the Brontës. He was surprised that such a popular destination had no rail connection and proposed a branch running from the Midland Railway's station at Keighley to Oxenhope. The line would also have stations at Ingrow, Damems, Oakworth and Haworth along the way. As with many little-used branch lines it was closed to passenger traffic in 1962, but rescued by heritage rail enthusiasts and reopened in 1968. Today it carries more than 100,000 passengers a year in a variety of steam and diesel locomotives and vintage carriages.

Not surprisingly, it makes regular appearances on screen and apart from standing in for Birmingham New Street has represented stations as far apart as Cheltenham and Glasgow. However the line's most famous appearance was not in *Peaky Blinders*, but the 1970 film *The*

ABOVE LEFT AND RIGHT
Vintage colour schemes and signage, make Keighley an attractive destination for period dramas.

RIGHT
The Keighley and Worth Valley Railway has separate platforms at Keighley Station.

FAR RIGHT
Oakworth Station is a popular tourist destination and featured in *The Railway Children*.

Railway Children starring Jenny Agutter. Oakworth was used as the local station and producers chose the line because, unlike any other heritage rail line of the time, it had a tunnel. Today, you can still travel to Haworth by rail, race down the platform at Oakworth and utter Jenny Agutter's heart-tugging line, "Daddy, my daddy" or stand on the spot in Keighley where Arthur endured his own heartbreaking moment.

BOLTON ABBEY
NORTH YORKSHIRE

One of the most memorable early scenes in *Peaky Blinders* comes in episode two of the first series, when Tommy, John and Arthur drive into the countryside to see their old friend Johnny Dogs. Johnny has pitched his caravan with the Lee family and has a white horse that Tommy has his eye on. In a beautiful riverside setting they toss coins to see if Tommy gets the horse, or Johnny gets the car.

With the matter resolved, members of the Lee family make a remark about Tommy's gypsy heritage and that's never going to be the prelude to some friendly banter. The ensuing fight sets the Lee family at war against the Shelbys, something only a marriage will fix.

The location for the riverside confrontation was on the banks of the river Wharfe in Yorkshire near the ruins of Bolton Priory. Although the Blinders do film in Bolton, Lancashire; Bolton Abbey is a village (and priory) in North Yorkshire, near the southern edge of the Yorkshire Dales National Park. The large estate is owned and run by the Duke of Devonshire, who also happens to be the owner of the magnificent Chatsworth House, where upper-crust horse trainer May Carleton is forever itching to put a fire in the guest bedroom.

Bolton Abbey estate is open to the public with many extra things to do apart from stand on the spot where the Blinders fell out with the Lees.

ABOVE LEFT
It was all going so well until one oft the Lees makes a remark about Tommy's mum.

ABOVE
The beautiful River Wharfe in Yorkshire, winds around Bolton Priory. The fight took place on the far bank.

Visitors can wander around the ruins of the 13th-century Bolton Priory, keep their balance walking across the 60 stone steps across the River Wharfe, visit the 600-year-old Laund Oak (now recumbent after 2016) or enjoy a stroll through Strid Wood. In 1810 the 6th Duke of Devonshire and the Reverend William Carr created paths and trails through the woods for the public to enjoy. And for Arthur Shelby there is always the Valley of Desolation – so named after a storm in 1826 which brought down many great trees – where he can contemplate his life. The valley gives access to Barden Fell and Barden Moor for the more serious walker.

PORTSOY
ABERDEENSHIRE

It's December 1933 when we rejoin the Shelbys in Series 6 and Tommy is visiting Miquelon, a French island off the coast of Newfoundland. It shouldn't be a surprise that the Shelby Company is operating in the area, in a previous conversation with Alfie Solomons, Tommy mentions Nova Scotia as one of the routes for his whisky into the American market.

But the creation of Miquelon is no work of fiction. Just 12 miles off the coast of Newfoundland, St. Pierre and Miquelon are two islands that are still part of French overseas territory today, administering French laws, regulating its French citizens. And as the drama

reveals, the islands suffered a massive drop in prosperity when Prohibition ended in 1933 and the import of alcohol into the United States became a legitimate business. The islanders had to return to the far less lucrative fishing industry. Tommy arrives for a meeting with Michael and his American backers at the Hotel Robert and makes a strong impression on the locals, before sitting down to propose a deal.

The village that *Peaky Blinders* used to create Miquelon was Portsoy in Aberdeenshire, on the north-east coast of Scotland. It was a perfect fit in terms of authenticity, as the real-life Miquelon is not far from Nova Scotia

(New Scotland), named because it looked like the Old Scotia. Portsoy harbour is the oldest on the Moray Firth and dates to the 17th century. It plays host to the annual Scottish Traditional Boat Festival at the end of June and beginning of July.

When the production crew arrived in a cold and snowy February of 2021 they were put up in Cullen's Seafield Arms Hotel, Portsoy's Dunn House and the Station Hotel, which will surely see an increase in business with Peaky fans keen to visit the island of Miquelon. While in the village they can enjoy a visit to the Shore Inn which posed as the Hotel Lanaan for the five days of filming and whose windows are considerably cleaner today. And a lot less French.

TOP
Two views of the pretty fishing village of Portsoy, a perfect fit for the island of Miquelon.

LEFT
The set decorators left their mark on Portsoy's buildings, such as this advert for Monsieur Brieau's boucherie.

MEOLS HALL
LANCASHIRE

Meols Hall near Southport on the Lancashire coast was very much in evidence in Series 3 of *Peaky Blinders* as a stand-in for Wilderness House in the grounds of Hampton Court. Wilderness was once the home of the Royal Gardener and its occupants included the great landscaper Lancelot 'Capability' Brown. Creator Steven Knight often likes to weave in historical fact to the background of the story, and the grace-and-favour house near the River Thames was indeed the home of a Russian Duchess exiled after the Revolution. Except Xenia Romanov, unlike *Peaky*'s Izabella Romanov, had to flee the country with very few possessions and certainly no store of jewels. Xenia was the sister of the last Tsar and was rescued by a British warship from the Crimea in 1919. In 1925 she moved into Frogmore Cottage on the Windsor Estate, at one time occupied by the Duke and Duchess of Sussex before their move to North America. It wasn't until 1936 that the Grand Duchess moved in to Wilderness House where she lived out her days until her death in 1960.

Meols Hall has had a more consistent occupation – it has been in the Hesketh family for 27 generations. The prize possession of the house, which is open to visitors between August and September (check Historic Houses Association for details), are the coronation chairs of Charles II from 1660. Parts of the house date to 1194 and the landscape has changed quite a bit in that time, because it was originally close to the coast. The sea once lapped against a small pier next to the Meols Hall gates. However, time and tide, and most effectively, the prevailing wind, have swept sand from Formby to build up land around Churchtown. For those looking for a wedding or conference venue in a *Peaky Blinders* location – look no further.

ABOVE
Meols Hall is a major location in Series 3.

RIGHT
Alfie Solomons and Cyril await their fate at an unusually 'sand duney' Margate.

FORMBY
LANCASHIRE

Formby, north of Liverpool, is famous for its sand dunes and wildlife reserve, its golf courses – Open Golf venue Royal Birkdale is nearby – and being the home of many Liverpool footballers over the years. It is also the town where the first official lifeboat was introduced in 1776 by William Hutchison, using a local Mersey gig for rescues. In the 21st century the Formby dunes have become famous as the stand-in for Margate on the North Kent coast and the showdown between Alfie Solomons and Tommy Shelby. Alfie is dying of cancer and brings his dog Cyril along, asking Tommy to take care of him before the final gunfight at the end of Series 4. Tommy says he won't, but it was a relief to many (and surely a signal of Alfie's passing) when Cyril appears at the beginning of Series 5.

BELOW
There is an important nature reserve in the sand dunes of Formby.

ASHTON MEMORIAL

LANCASTER

The Ashton Memorial dominates the Lancaster skyline. At around 150 feet (50m) tall you can get a great view of the Lancashire countryside and across to Morecambe Bay from its terraces. Although it looks a little like Sacré-Cœur in Paris, it has been dubbed 'England's Taj Mahal of the North', because like the great Indian mausoleum built in memory of Mumtaz Mahal, wealthy Lancaster industrialist Lord Ashton commissioned it in memory of his late wife Jessy.

The interior was used as the setting for the memorable scene in the first episode of Series 6, when Tommy Shelby comes to meet Gina Gray who is drinking heavily, playing loud jazz and tells the head of the Shelby Company it's 'no deal' selling white powder to Uncle Jack. Set designers placed Gina's bar in front of one of the many alcoves, while the central space – used today for weddings and civil ceremonies – was filled with vintage thirties furniture, around which the two characters circled in a scene crackling with tension.

The Ashton Memorial was built using Portland Stone, with a domed copper roof and Cornish granite steps. It sits in 54 acres of Williamson Park to the east of Lancaster. The site was reclaimed from moorland and first developed in the 1860s, using unemployed cotton spinners. During the American Civil War (1861-1865), when Union forces blockaded the cotton exporting ports of the South, Lancashire's weaving industry suffered a 'cotton famine'

and workers were forced to find other employment. The park was developed by James Williamson Snr, father of Lord Ashton. It was handed over to Lancaster Corporation by Lord Ashton in 1881, though the grand memorial to his wife was not built until 1909.

Today, it is owned and run by Lancaster City Council, and entrance to the park and the memorial is free.

TOP
The stunning floor is in black, white and red marble.

RIGHT
Gina Gray's 'jazz salon' can be viewed through the arched window.